First World War
and Army of Occupation
War Diary
France, Belgium and Germany

27 DIVISION
Divisional Troops
129 Brigade Royal Field Artillery
26 August 1915 - 26 December 1915

WO95/2257/6

The Naval & Military Press Ltd
www.nmarchive.com
Published in association with The National Archives

Published by

The Naval & Military Press Ltd

Unit 10 Ridgewood Industrial Park,

Uckfield, East Sussex,

TN22 5QE England

Tel: +44 (0) 1825 749494

www.naval-military-press.com

www.nmarchive.com

This diary has been reprinted in facsimile from the original. Any imperfections are inevitably reproduced and the quality may fall short of modern type and cartographic standards.

© Crown Copyright
Images reproduced by permission of The National Archives, London, England, 2015.

Contents

Document type	Place/Title	Date From	Date To
Heading	WO95/2257/6		
Heading	27 Div Troops 129 Bde RFA 1915 Aug-1915 Dec		
Heading	27th Division 129th Bde R.F.A. Vol I Aug & Sept 15		
War Diary	Armentieres	26/08/1915	18/09/1915
War Diary	Cerisy	19/09/1915	30/09/1915
Heading	129th Bde. R.F.A. Oct-Dec Vol III		
Heading	27th Division 129th Bde R.F.A. Oct 1915 Vol II		
War Diary	Froissy	01/10/1915	29/10/1915
War Diary	Ailly Sur Somme	01/11/1915	06/12/1915
War Diary	Villers Bocage	19/12/1915	24/12/1915
War Diary	Marseilles	26/12/1915	26/12/1915

W005/225716

29 DIV TROOPS

129 BDE RFA

1915 AUG — 1915 DEC

4555

121/7740

34th Division

129th Bde H.Q.

Vol 1.

Aug & Sept 15

Army Form C. 2118

456

129th (Howitzer) Brigade R.F.A.

WAR DIARY
or
INTELLIGENCE SUMMARY.
(Erase heading not required.)

Instructions regarding War Diaries and Intelligence Summaries are contained in F.S. Regs. Part II. and the Staff Manual respectively. Title pages will be prepared in manuscript.

Place	Date	Hour	Summary of Events and Information	Remarks and references to Appendices
ARMENTIERES	1915 Aug 26.		On the formation of the 129th (Howitzer) Brigade R.F.A. the following details arrived from England and joined the 27th Divisional Artillery:— 1 Warrant Officer, 23 NCOs and men RFA. 1 NCO Army Ordnance Corps and 5 NCOs Army Veterinary Corps.	WRe
	29th		2 men from Q Battery R.H.A.	
	29th		Major H.R. EDEN B.S.O. R.H.A. was appointed to the Command of the Brigade 2nd Lieut M.I. WAYTE R.F.A. was appointed Orderly Officer	WSee
			Lieut S.A. ROBSON R.F.A.(T) 27th Divisional Ammunition Column appointed Acting Adjutant	one
	Sepr 1st		The Brigade was formed of the following Batteries which became designated as stated below	
	6th		A Battery 53rd Brigade became A Battery 129th Brigade Officers Major D.C. SPENCER SMITH Lieut S.J. PUSINELLI " M TROUTON " DN HOSSIE	
			A Battery 92nd Brigade became B Battery 129th Brigade Officers Captn M.R.C. NANSON 2nd/Lieut B.J.T. ~~Somers~~ PICKTHALL " E.W.M. PROTHEROE " M.H. LUSHINGTON	

Army Form C. 2118

WAR DIARY
or
INTELLIGENCE SUMMARY

129th (Howitzer) Brigade RFA

(Erase heading not required.)

Instructions regarding War Diaries and Intelligence Summaries are contained in F.S. Regs., Part II. and the Staff Manual respectively. Title pages will be prepared in manuscript.

Place	Date	Hour	Summary of Events and Information	Remarks and references to Appendices
ARMENTIERES	1915 Sept 6th		C Battery 6th Brigade became C Battery 129th Brigade. Officer Capt Hon I.M. FIENNES. Major A SUTHERLAND " " R H CLARKE " " E BROWN	WD
	9th 6th & 14th		All 3 Batteries are in action within 1 & 3 miles E - S E of ARMENTIÈRES with Wagon Lines near ERQUINGHEM. 6 Drivers joined C Battery. The Brigade came under the orders of the B.G.R.A. Coy 8th Divl Artillery and during this period registration was carried out daily upon enemy trenches and tactical points opposite the 8th Division front.	WD
	14th		The Batteries were relieved in action by Batteries of 20th Division and the Brigade went back to billets in farms about 2 mile West of BAILLEUL.	WD
	16th & 18th		The Brigade was moved by train to a new Area taken over by 27th Division East of AMIENS. The rail journey occupying about 9 hours.	WD
CERISY	19th & 20th		The Brigade arrived at CERISY and was billeted there.	WD
"	18th		CAPT. M. BOLLAM was appointed to command the Brigade Ammunition Column which has been formed as a separate Unit from Section previously attached to the Batteries. The other Officer of the Column is Lieut N.A. HOUSTON R.F.A.	WD
"	18th		Major F.G. BUSHNELL R.A.M.C. (T) assumes medical charge of the Brigade.	WD

458

Army Form C. 2118.

WAR DIARY
or
INTELLIGENCE SUMMARY.
(Erase heading not required.)

Instructions regarding War Diaries and Intelligence Summaries are contained in F. S. Regs., Part II. and the Staff Manual respectively. Title pages will be prepared in manuscript.

Place	Date	Hour	Summary of Events and Information	Remarks and references to Appendices
CERISY	1915 Sept 22-23		One Section of B Battery occupied the height on a position in the edge of a wood about 900 yards E of CHUIGNES, as put N of the CHUIGNES - FONTAINE- les- CAPPY road. One Section of C Battery occupied during the night a position in a valley 1½ mile E of CAPPY, and just S of the CAPPY - HERECOURT road.	WRc
	23rd		Brigade Head Quarters, "A" Battery, and remainder of B & C Batteries close to the Canal bridge on the CHUIGNOLLES - BRAY road.	
	"	P.M. 3 - 3.30	Section of B Battery fired 100 Rounds on portion of Enemy's front trench. Ray 18.00	
		5 - 5.30	Section of "C" " " 100 " on " " " 28.00	WRc
			" " " " " " mine heads " 10.00	
	24th	P.M. 2.30 - 3	Section of "B" Battery " 200 " on portion of Enemy front trench " 20.00	WRc
		4.30 - 5	Section of "C" Battery " 200 " " " " " " 25.00	
	25.		Section of B & C Batteries to active came under the orders for tactical purposes of the O.C. A & B Group respectively of the 27th Division front. Column moved up to a position in Vallon S of MORCOURT Brigade Ammunition.	WRc
	26th 27th 30th		B Battery fired 12 Rounds on the Enemy's Trenches Section 60½ to 51½ at Ranges varying from 2000 to 2800 in retaliation to a Minenwerfer bombardment on trenches C Battery fired 38 Rounds of Lyddite on various points on the Enemy Trenches at ranges varying from 2075 to 8075.	WRc

104th Bde. R.F.A.
Oct — Dec / 1902 III

459

121/7551

27th Koracin

129th Bde. R.F.A.

Oct 1915

Vol II

443

Army Form C. 2118.

WAR DIARY
or
INTELLIGENCE SUMMARY.
(Erase heading not required.)

Place	Date	Hour	Summary of Events and Information	Remarks and references to Appendices
FROISSY	1915 Oct 1		"A" Battery 117 Brigade 26th Division took up a position adjoining C129 B.F. and were attached to them for instructional purposes. Also section of B.117 took up a position adjoining and were attached to B.129 for the same purpose for one week.	WRE
	Oct 1st to 10th		The Brigade ammunition column moved back to Billets at Cerisy. "B" Battery fired 56 rounds Shrapnel and 17 rounds Hy adite on Enemys Trenches and communication trenches in rear at ranges 2000 to 2500 yds Partly at request of Infantry in retaliation to the Enemys shelling our Trenches and partly for Registration purposes. "C" Battery also fired 41 rounds of Hy adite on various points on Enemys trenches at ranges varying from 3900 to 5150 yards for the same purpose as "B" By	WRE
	11th		A.129 Battery moved back to CERISY from FROISSY	WRE
	12th to 20th		B/129 By fired 65 rounds of Shrapnel, at ranges varying from 4800 – 5000 yds on Enemys trenches opposite BOUCHER and CARPEZAT woods, partly for Registration purposes and partly in Retaliation to Enemys fire which showed considerable activity at times	

2353 Wt. W3411/1454 700,000 5/15 D.D.&L. A.D.S.S./Forms/C. 2118.

Army Form C. 2118

460

WAR DIARY
or
INTELLIGENCE SUMMARY
(Erase heading not required.)

Instructions regarding War Diaries and Intelligence Summaries are contained in F. S. Regs., Part II. and the Staff Manual respectively. Title pages will be prepared in manuscript.

Place	Date	Hour	Summary of Events and Information	Remarks and references to Appendices
FROISSY	OCTOBER 12th to 20th		C.129 Battery fired 6 Rounds of Shrapnel on Enemy's Trenches in Retaliation to Minenwerfer at range of 4500 yds.	/MC
	21st		B & C. 129 Batteries came out of action and returned to their Wagon Lines at FROISSY.	/MC
	23rd	10AM	Brigade Head Quarters, "B" & "C" Batteries marched from FROISSY to CERISY where they joined "A" Battery and the ammunition Column.	/MC
	24th	1 PM	The Brigade marched from CERISY to BOVES a distance of about 17 miles arriving there at about 6. P.M.	/MC
	25th	9.30AM	The Brigade marched from BOVES to AILLY SUR SOMME a distance of about 10 miles arriving there at 3.30 P.M.	/MC
	27th		a draft of 7 Drivers and one Gunner, arrived from the BASE.	/MC
	29th		MAJOR. W. R. EDEN. D.S.O. commanding the Brigade, was gazetted Tempy. LIEUT. COL.	/MC

Army Form C. 2118.

WAR DIARY
or
INTELLIGENCE SUMMARY
(Erase heading not required.)

Instructions regarding War Diaries and Intelligence Summaries are contained in F. S. Regs., Part II. and the Staff Manual respectively. Title pages will be prepared in manuscript.

Place	Date	Hour	Summary of Events and Information	Remarks and references to Appendices
AILLY SUR SOMME	1.11.15		7 Gunners joined the Brigade.	nil
	3.		Captn. G.L.C. WHITE joined the Brigade to command B Battery, vice Captn. M.R.C. NANSON posted to 21st Division.	nil
	3		2ND LIEUT C.S.RICH was posted to "B" Battery of the Brigade.	nil
	7		A Draft of 5 Gunners arrived for the Brigade.	nil
	10		Major D.C. SPENCER SMITH of "A" Battery was posted to "K" Battery RHA	nil
	10		Major J.G.C. THOMPSON of the 27th Divisional Ammunition Column joined the Brigade to command "A" Battery, vice Major De SPENCER SMITH.	nil
	11		A Draft of 26 N.C.O's & men joined from the Base.	nil
	14		A Draft of 9 N.C.O.s were posted to the Brigade from various Batteries of R.H.A.	nil
	19		A Draft of 13 Gunner Drivers joined the Brigade & were posted to the Ammunition Column from the 1st Brigade R.F.A.	nil

Army Form C. 2118.

WAR DIARY
or
~~INTELLIGENCE SUMMARY~~
(Erase heading not required.)

Instructions regarding War Diaries and Intelligence Summaries are contained in F. S. Regs., Part II. and the Staff Manual respectively. Title pages will be prepared in manuscript.

Place	Date	Hour	Summary of Events and Information	Remarks and references to Appendices
AILLY-SUR-SOMME	6/12/15		The Brigade marched from AILLY-SUR-SOMME to VILLIERS-BOCAGE a distance of about 8 miles.	We
VILLIERS-BOCAGE	19/12/15		Field Marshall Sir J. French on relinquishing command of the British Forces in France passed along the main road near VILLIERS BOCAGE, the Brigade lined the road to cheer him as he passed.	We
	24/12/15		The Brigade entrained at LONGEAU for MARSEILLES.	We
MARSEILLES	26/12/15		The Brigade arrived at MARSEILLES and moved into camp. Head Quarters, C Battery and the ammunition column at LES ABATTOIRS. A Battery and B Battery at LA VALENTINE	We

www.ingramcontent.com/pod-product-compliance
Lightning Source LLC
Chambersburg PA
CBHW081253170426
43191CB00037B/2148